Sheep

Beverley Randell

Contents

All sorts of sheep

Most sheep have white wool.
Their wool can be dyed,
and made into
clothes like these.

Some sheep are
brown
or grey
or black,
and their wool
does not need
to be dyed.

Many sheep like the dry hills, but some like flat land.

Some sheep have very strong wool, and this is good for making carpets.

What are some carpets made from?

Rams, ewes and lambs

A male sheep
is called a ram.
Many rams have
big curly horns, and
all rams have hard heads.
Rams butt each other.

Some carpets are made
from very strong wool.

A female sheep is called a ewe.
Sheep grow up fast.
A ewe can have her first lamb
when she is only one year old.

What is a male sheep called?

Young lambs

Most lambs are born in the spring.

Many ewes have twin lambs, and some have triplets (three at once)

A male sheep is called a ram.

Lambs can walk
soon after they are born.
A new little lamb has to stand
so that it can get
its first drink of milk.
When lambs drink
they wag their tails.
Young lambs run and jump
and chase each other.

Can ewes have three lambs at once?

Wool and meat

Farmers keep sheep
because of their wool.
Wool is shorn from the sheep
in the shearing shed.

Yes. Ewes can have three lambs at once.

Sheep don't need their wool
in the hot summer.
They look thin when their wool

has just
been shorn,
but it soon
grows again.

Farmers
keep sheep
for meat, too.

Why do farmers keep sheep?

Food for sheep

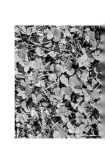

All sheep eat grass and clover.

Sheep nibble short grass.

They can eat the short grass that grows on dry hillsides.

Farmers keep sheep
because of their wool and their meat.

When grass and clover
stop growing in the winter,
sheep are fed
sweet-smelling hay.

Sheep chew the cud,
just as cattle do.

Some sheep eat
vegetables, too.

What do sheep eat?

Caring for ewes and lambs

Some hill sheep can take care of themselves, but many farmers help the ewes at lambing time. Lambs and ewes can die in cold weather. If a mother ewe dies, the farmer will try to give her lamb to another ewe. The smell of the new lamb has to be just right.

Sheep eat grass, clover and hay.
Some sheep eat vegetables.

If the ewe keeps pushing
the lamb away,
someone has to feed it milk
from a bottle.
Farm children often have
pet lambs to feed.

Do lambs die in cold weather?

A long time ago

The first wild sheep
lived in Europe and Central Asia,
where the winters are very cold.
Their wool kept them warm.

Wild sheep are like goats,
and they can run down
steep hillsides.

Yes. Some lambs die in cold weather.

Wolves used to hunt
the wild sheep, and
the sheep learned to run away.

Sheep on farms
will run away from dogs, too.
Dogs and wolves look alike.

What animals used to hunt wild sheep?

Sheep farmers need sheep dogs

Sheep farmers and shepherds
need good dogs.
The farmer trains his dogs
to help him move the sheep
from one place to another.
Well-trained dogs are clever.

Wolves used to hunt wild sheep.